Welcome to the Lord's Table:

Book for Communicants

Revised Edition

Writers: Herbert F. Brokering
Michael C. D. McDaniel

Editor: Marvin L. Roloff

Artist: RKB Studio

Prepared for the Boards of Parish Education of the Lutheran Church in America, The Lutheran Church—Missouri Synod, and The American Lutheran Church.

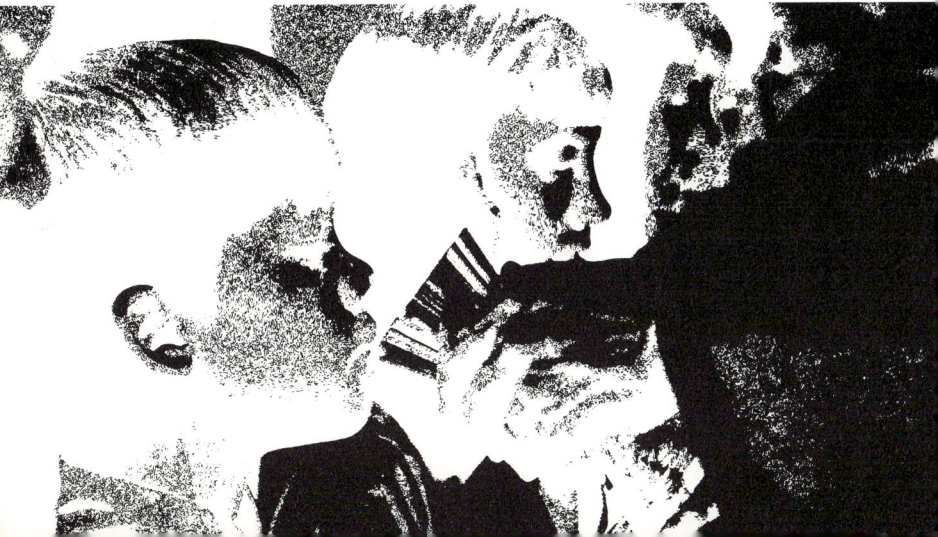

What do you think about when you hear the words Holy Communion?

Why do you think about these things? Which words describe Holy Communion for you?

Holy Communion means many things to many people. It has particular meaning for each one for personal reasons.

The names used for Holy Communion tell us something about the meaning of Communion. Some of these names are the Lord's Supper, Sacrament of the Altar, the Last Supper, Communion, and Eucharist.

We never know all there is to know about Holy Communion. We share our meanings of Holy Communion in the church.

What in the Scriptures comes to your mind when you think of Holy Communion?

Which story in the Old Testament? Who are the people in the story?

Which story in the New Testament? Who are the people in the story? Which part of Jesus' life is in the story? What does this tell you about Holy Communion?

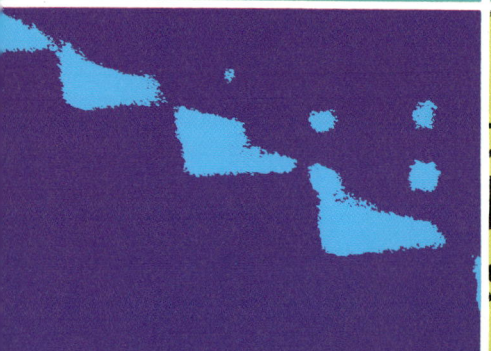

n the night
:ook bread, 24
hanks, he br
s my body v
in remembra

d the whole
8And they str
let robe upon
wn of thorns
nd put a reed
neeling before

The celebration of Holy Communion is a part of many biblical stories. It is important in many of the events in the Scriptures. It comes from the celebration of the Passover in the Old Testament. This story is written in Exodus 12:1-20. The story of Jesus in the Upper Room with his disciples is in the New Testament. It is written in Matthew 26:26-29, Mark 14:22-25, Luke 22:14-19, and 1 Corinthians 11:23-26. Jesus ate bread and wine with his disciples.

When we eat bread and wine in Holy Communion Jesus is present with us. God meets his people in Holy Communion.

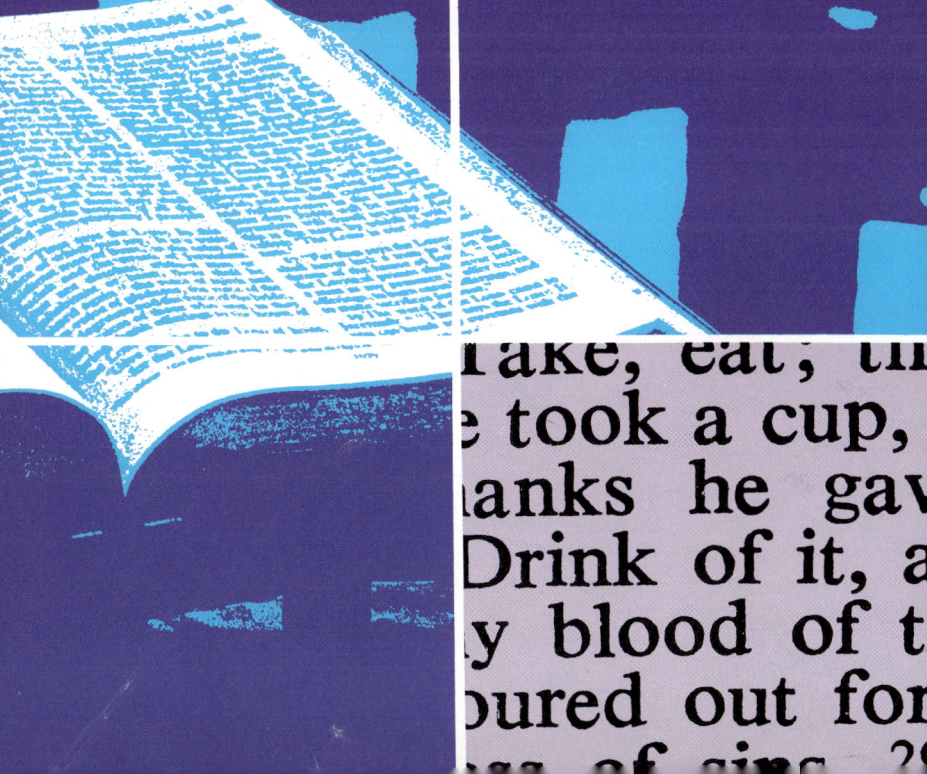

With whom would you like to come to Communion?

Would you invite them? Would they come with you? Why would you invite them? How could you do it? What does this say about Holy Communion?

Holy Communion is a meal for the family of God. Christ is present, joining us with God in Holy Communion.

We are all in the family of God. In Baptism we became members of the family. Now we are preparing to celebrate with one another. We will eat together. We are friends sharing Christ's love for us. We are God's family. Christ's love is powerful and holds us together.

Which way of setting the table looks most like Holy Communion?

Could all of these be Holy Communion? Why or why not? Which feels most like Communion? Which table setting can you picture yourself in? Why?

In Holy Communion we are at the table of the Lord. It is a great meal. It is being with Christ who is the host. It is a family meal. Communion means being together. It is talking with each other.

As a communion of people we are not alone. In this meal Christ is with us. Because we are together and Christ loves us, we are united with him and with each other.

Why is Holy Communion a meal of eating and drinking?

What does this say to you about Holy Communion? How important is eating and drinking? Why did Jesus use bread and wine? Why do we use bread and wine?

Holy Communion is eating and drinking. Food and drink are part of God's creation. They are what we need to live.

Jesus used bread and wine. It was the most common food in his day. Today we use these same foods in Holy Communion. Jesus is with us in the eating and drinking of Communion.

What experiences have you had in your life that remind you of Holy Communion?

Why do these experiences remind you of Holy Communion? How do these experiences help you understand Holy Communion?

Holy Communion is important in our daily lives.
Holy Communion is part of the way God cares for us,
his people. And we care for one another. It is a way
in which we experience the presence of Christ.
He is with us where we live.

What questions do you have about Holy Communion?

Who have you talked to about your questions? What have they told you? Who else can you talk to? What other concerns do you have about Holy Communion?

Holy Communion is the gathering of the family of God. We all come as children, having questions and concerns. Some of these are problems and they hurt. Some of them make us feel guilty and have doubts. Having questions and concerns is part of our being human. It is good to talk to people about them. It is good to talk to God in prayer about them.

God sent Christ to join us in Holy Communion. He comes where there is trouble and he brings us peace. Christ is with us always.

Why is Holy Communion joyful?

What is the most joyful part of Holy Communion to you? How can you express this joy?

Holy Communion is a gift. It is good to receive a gift. Holy Communion is a gift from God. The gift is love, forgiveness, joy, and peace. We are thankful for this gift.

Holy Communion is a joyful time. It is good news. So we are glad! We rejoice and shout! For God is with us!

The Story of Your Communion

Holy Communion is a celebration. It is a time to celebrate that God is with us. God's people have always celebrated and rejoiced because God is with them.

Our celebration of Holy Communion has a long history. It can be traced to its beginning in the Old Testament where God's people celebrated his presence with them.

Over three thousand years ago God rescued his people from slavery in Egypt through a great leader named Moses.

Moses begged the king (called the "Pharaoh") for many years to let the people of Israel leave Egypt. In spite of many signs which Moses gave to show that God wanted his people set free, the Pharaoh would not allow them to leave. Finally, Moses told his people that in the middle of the night death would come to every house in the land except the houses of the Israelites. All the men, women, and children were told to be dressed, stay ready throughout the night, and take only the possessions they could carry on their backs in order to get away quickly. Their supper was to be the meat of a lamb, and the blood of the lamb was to be put over their doors to mark the houses of God's Chosen People. Thus the "angel of death" would pass over their homes and visit only the Egyptian families.

In the great commotion which upset the nation that night because of deaths in every Egyptian house, Pharaoh sent word to let the Israelites go. Quickly they fled into the night, out of slavery in Egypt and on the road toward freedom in the promised land.

Every year since that night the people of Israel have come together in their homes to celebrate this event in a festival called the *Passover*. The meal eaten at Passover celebrations in Jewish families today brings back to life the covenant (the promise or agreement) which God made with his people on that night in Egypt so long ago. In remembrance and thanksgiving, men, women, and children celebrate the release from slavery—the salvation—which God promises to his people.

Coming safely out of Egypt, the people of God began a long journey through the wilderness toward a new land which God had promised to them. In spite of all the special signs of God's care for them, they were forever grumbling about their troubles, murmuring against God, and ungrateful for the salvation God had given them through Moses. Over and over again, the people turned away from God and did foolish things—even after Moses gave them two stone tablets engraved with the clear laws of God, the Ten Commandments.

Once in the "Promised Land," there was every reason for the Israelites to be faithful and obedient. They had God's law and they enjoyed his continual blessings. Yet the Israelites rebelled against God and broke the covenant with him. Despite God's blessing they were always ready to make an idol or false god of anything which satisfied their foolish desires. Although freed from slavery to the Egyptians, people were still slaves to sin.

But God was with them all the time and did not give up. In spite of their sins, God inspired prophet after prophet to tell the people the truth and remind them of God's covenant with them. Yet it was clear that just knowing God's laws did not give people the power to keep his Commandments, and they broke his covenant time after time.

The prophets brought a message that some day God would establish a new covenant and make his people great again. But the people never really understood the prophets. Instead they hoped that God would restore them to the greatness they had when David was king.

Through long dark years there were always some people in Israel who hoped in their hearts that God would bring back peace and justice. Would their prayers be heard? What would God do?

God did come to his people, but in an unexpected way. He chose to be born as a human and live among people— sharing their lives, speaking their language, sympathizing with their heartaches, and knowing their hopes. He came as the baby Jesus, born in a manger.

Jesus spent his life telling people about their heavenly Father and his great love for them. He spoke to all people, speaking the truth about God, wanting no glory for himself.

On the evening before Jesus was crucified in Jerusalem he invited his disciples to eat the Passover feast with him. They gathered at the table in the upper room of a friend's house. Jesus and his disciples had eaten meals together many times before this. However, this meal was a very special one, a gift which Jesus gave to his disciples and he gives to us.

Jesus gave his disciples bread and wine in the Upper Room.

At supper the night he was betrayed,
our Lord Jesus took some bread in his hands;
and then, when he had given thanks to [God],
he broke it and gave it to his friends.
And he said, "Take this, and eat it:
This is my body; it is given for you:
Do this to remember me."
After supper he took a cup of wine
and after giving thanks, he gave it to them.
And he said, "Drink from this, all of you:
This cup is God's new covenant in my blood
which is poured out for you and for all mankind
for the forgiveness of sins.
Whenever you drink from it from now on,
do this to remember me."

(Taken from *Contemporary Worship 2—The Holy Communion*)

By giving his disciples bread and wine, Jesus was joining them in a wonderful and mysterious way, sharing his body and blood in the bread and wine.

This Last Supper which Jesus shared with his disciples was a new covenant. It took the place of the old covenant which God had made with the Israelites at the time of the exodus from Egypt.

Instead of the body and blood of the Passover lamb, Jesus' own body and blood was sacrificed. Jesus is the lamb of God who died for us, so that we can be free from the power of sin and death just as the Israelites were freed by God from the power of the Pharaoh of Egypt.

"The Lord's Supper" is the name of the new covenant meal. It reminds us that it is the Lord himself who invites us, provides this meal, and welcomes us to his table. Here Christ gives us himself with the bread and wine as he did to the disciples.

It is also called "Holy Communion." This stresses the community or fellowship which Christ's body and blood create, bringing all men together in the forgiveness of sins and the power of Jesus' new life.

Called the "Eucharist" it describes the great thanksgiving we have for this gift of God.

Holy Communion is also called the Sacrament of the Altar, as the bread and wine are received at an altar.

Our joy in Holy Communion begins in Baptism where we enter the fellowship of the church. Baptism is a sacrament. It is a special act through which we become children of God. Baptism, in which water is used in the name of God, is like a new birth, making one a member of God's family.

Once we have been baptized, we never need it again. But our faith or trust in God needs food to keep it alive. That is why Christians hear God's Word as often as they can, come together for worship, and celebrate the sacrament of the Lord's Supper.

There are just two sacraments—Holy Baptism and the Lord's Supper. In Baptism we become God's children. The Lord's Supper is given to us to give us strength. Our bodies need food in order to keep strong. Our faith also needs strengthening. Through his Word and through the Lord's Supper, God is reminding us that we are his children. Through his Word, the Bible, and through the Lord's Supper God encourages us to believe that we are his children and that we are forgiven.

God chose a simple meal for this Sacrament of Holy Communion. It is a meal that Christians want to take part in just as

often as they can. Since it is God's victory celebration—victory over sin and death—it is a happy and joyous kind of action. What is happier than a family feast? The Lord's Table is like a great feast, a wonderful dinner party, or a special celebration. But it is not really like any of these. It is far more wonderful, for each time we are reminded that some day we will all be together forever with the Lord who is our host at this feast.

Eating together is one of the friendliest things people ever do. It is a wonderful time to understand each other better, to talk about things which we are doing, plan for tomorrow, and work out problems which we have. Hopes, sorrows, joys, and troubles are shared when people eat together, and there is a warm feeling of belonging which we cannot feel anywhere else. Holy Communion is a happy meal that brings us forgiveness, life, and salvation.

At the Lord's Table friends meet in love and joy, and have the closest possible union with Jesus, sharing not only food and drink but also thoughts, wishes, and feelings. Those who meet at the Lord's Table know that they belong to each other and are all very much wanted there.

Have you ever been invited to eat at the table of some wonderful friend and share his meal? Such an invitation means that you are really liked and wanted. Everywhere in God's kingdom — every communion table in every church —

Jesus is as much alive today as he was in the Upper Room with his disciples, and he invites everyone to come eat the bread of new life and drink the wine of salvation. Nothing on earth can compare with the communion, the belonging, of those who share in this celebration.

Nothing is like the joy we have in Communion, because we know God loves and forgives us.

To this great and everlasting banquet, God himself invites you. Your place at his table is ready.